# ARE YOU MOMMY MATERIAL?

Y ou've told your kids about the starving little children of Slobovia who would give anything for such a nice plateful of sesame turnip balls. You've talked until your face turned blue about the hideous effects of not eating liver. But it's still possible that your little darlings might be getting less than the minimum daily requirement of guilt. To make sure that you're feeding your kids' neuroses right, take this Good Mother Aptitude Test:

—Is your idea of a persuasive argument, "Do it because I said so" or "because I'm the mother, *that's* why"?
—Do you know how many peas a child must eat to qualify for one Ho-Ho?
—Do you regularly remind your kids: "You'll be sorry when I'm six feet under" or "This will hurt me more than it hurts you"?
—If your child starts sniveling when you insist he eat his beans, can you be counted on to say, "If you don't stop crying, I'll really give you something to cry about"?

If you've answered YES to most of these questions, relax—you've come through the Good Mother Aptitude Test with flying colors. Keep up the good work—someday they'll thank you for it!

---

NORMA PETERSON is a prize-winning journalist whose articles have appeared in *McCall's, Reader's Digest,* and *USA Today.* ART PETERSON, her husband, teaches high school in San Francisco and is the author of *Teachers,* an uproarious field guide to strange birds who flock to the pedagogical business, which is available in a Plume edition. The parents of two children, the Petersons have learned by experience that a mother's most heartfelt wish really does come true: Your own kids invariably *do* behave just as badly as you did when you were a child.

# The
# *Unofficial*
# M O T H E R ' S
# *Handbook*

## Norma and Art Peterson

### Illustrations by Cindy Chan

A PLUME BOOK

## NEW AMERICAN LIBRARY

A DIVISION OF PENGUIN BOOKS USA INC., NEW YORK

PUBLISHED IN CANADA BY
PENGUIN BOOKS CANADA LIMITED, MARKHAM, ONTARIO

PLUME TRADEMARK REG. U.S. PAT. OFF. AND FOREIGN COUNTRIES
REGISTERED TRADEMARK—MARCA REGISTRADA
HECHO EN BRATTLEBORO, VT.

SIGNET, SIGNET CLASSIC, MENTOR, ONYX, PLUME, MERIDIAN and NAL BOOKS are published *in the United States* by NEW AMERICAN LIBRARY, a division of Penguin Books USA Inc.,
1633 Broadway, New York, New York 10019,
*in Canada* by Penguin Books Canada Limited, 2801 John Street, Markham, Ontario L3R 1B4

**Library of Congress Cataloging-in-Publication Data**

Peterson, Norma.
   The unofficial mother's handbook / Norma and Art Peterson.
      p.     cm.
   ISBN 0-452-26246-1
   1. Mothers—Humor.   I. Peterson, Art.   II. Title.
PN6231.M68P48   1989
818'.5402—dc19                                                88-36831
                                                             CIP

First Printing, April, 1989

1   2   3   4   5   6   7   8   9

PRINTED IN THE UNITED STATES OF AMERICA

# *Contents*

# CONTENTS

# 7 MOM'S PHOTO ALBUM      *109*

# 8 JOKES FOR MOMS WHO NEED THEM      *121*

*To Brendan and Elizabeth*

# Acknowledgments

This book would not have been possible if we had not had the cooperation of mothers who were careful observers and articulate story-tellers. We are grateful to the following moms:

Aurelia Brown, Denise Brown, Elizabeth Crews, Judy Foreman, Rachel Hendricks, Pat Hultgren, Dixie Jordan, Lori Lusted, Abigail Marshall, Gloria McGarry, Carole Terwilliger Meyers, Terry Nagle, Monica O'Kane, Joanna Pearlman, Gail Peterson, Lisa Rosenthal, Debbie Saunders, and Susan Skov.

# The
## Unofficial
# MOTHER'S
## Handbook

# 1

# *Are You Mother Material?*

T*ime flies. One day you are making your infant child an offer she is in no position to refuse: "Duzzee beebee wanna kissee?" Before you know it, twenty-six years have passed, and you are on the phone to the same child asking, "Are we ever going to get a chance to see our grandson?"*

*Along the way, you'll have a lot of other questions. During the early years, a favorite will be: "Can't you hold it until you get home?" Later there'll be: "What do you mean there's nothing to do?" And eventually: "Do you have any idea what time it is, young lady?"*

*The answers, and the mothering experiences with which they are connected, will whiz by so quickly the whole adventure can become a blur. So let's slow down the projector and look at some of what's in store for you one frame at a time, beginning with a question no one may ever have had the nerve to ask: Are you good mother material?*

# GMAT (The Good Mother Aptitude Test)

1. **You prefer to spend a vacation:**
   - (A) Sunning on the Côte d'Azur
   - (B) Skiing the high season at St. Moritz
   - (C) Cooking hot dogs at Fanny's Family Camper Park

2. **Your favorite topic of conversation is:**
   - (A) Elizabeth Taylor's love life
   - (B) Insider trading
   - (C) Doo-doo

3. **Your idea of wild spontaneous fun is:**
   - (A) Skinny-dipping at midnight in a fountain in Rome
   - (B) Making love on the Capitol steps
   - (C) Calling a baby-sitter the same day as the PTA pot luck

4. **The headline most likely to catch your attention would be:**
   - (A) Mideast Factions Kiss and Make Up; Agree on Everything
   - (B) Polyester Found to Cure Cancer
   - (C) One-Night Record: New Mom Gets Six Hours Straight Sleep

5. **You want your kid to share his Dr. Wacko doll with a friend. The most persuasive argument would be:**
   - (A) Wouldn't you want me and Mr. Rogers to be proud of you?
   - (B) You know how Daddy is always telling you there are a finite number of resources in the world and that they can only be fairly allocated through a cooperative system.
   - (C) Do it because I said so.

6. **Your definition of a truly tolerant woman is one who:**
   - (A) Admires her husband's thoughtfulness when he takes his secretary to lunch
   - (B) Listens respectfully to a telephone pitchman who calls at dinnertime
   - (C) Smiles when, after $15,000 of ballet and piano lessons, her child takes up playing bongo drums in a Hawaiian punk band

7. **The most important question to ask when making dinner reservations at a pricey restaurant is:**
   (A) Do you have valet parking?
   (B) Do you serve Côte de Nuits burgundy at room temperature?
   (C) Do you have waterproof booster seats?

8. **Finish the following statement: The world would be a better place if we would just**
   (A) Free all political prisoners
   (B) Pray more
   (C) Stop fighting over who took whose Choc-o-Bliss

9. **To be well-rounded, a mother needs to know:**
   (A) That *Così Fan Tutte* is an opera, not an ice cream flavor
   (B) The difference between Manet and Monet
   (C) What happened to the Itsy Bitsy Spider when it rained

10. **The best way to gain uncritical acceptance for your idea that mothering should be subsidized by government grants is to:**
    (A) Address the local Kiwanis
    (B) Call the Donahue show
    (C) Filibuster your six-month-old

ANSWERS: The correct answer in each case was "C." If you did poorly, don't despair. There will be plenty of opportunity for on-the-job training. Read on.

---

"How sharper than a serpant's (sic) tooth it is to have a thankless child."
—William Shakespeare

*(Wow. So even back then kids were forgetting Mother's Day.)*

---

**17**

## Can You Act Like a Mother?

Motherhood is partially instinctive. All mothers share the magical ability to divine when a child is faking a tummyache.

But possessing a measly one or two motherly traits won't get you very far in your eighteen-year-long endurance struggle with an adversary who is younger, cuter, and probably sneakier than you are. To measure up, you need no less than eleven basic mom characteristics. How many of the following apply to you?

### 1. You have a critical eye.

—When your daughter is elected president of her class at school, carrying every homeroom but one, do you want to know, "So why didn't they like you in Mrs. Ruckles's room?"

### 2. You enjoy being a martyr.

—Is your happiness at ironing your son's boxer shorts in ninety degree weather exceeded only by your delight in telling him about it?

### 3. You are immune to kids' fashions.

—Can you walk blithely past the Calvin Klein and Ralph Lauren and head straight for the sensible dorky stuff?

### 4. You have proper motherly pride.

—When your son pitches his first Little League game and walks all the players on the opposing team, can you brag, "Ah, what a son. No one could even get a hit against him."

### 5. You can make decisions with the confidence of a big league umpire.

—Do you always know who looked at who funny, who hid the Chee•tos, and whose turn it is to get the Smurf cup?

### 6. You have eyes in the back of your head.

—Does your sixth sense always tell you when someone is flushing a cat down a toilet?

18

### 7. You know the rules of nutrition.

—Do you know how many peas a person should be forced to eat to qualify for one Ho Ho?

### 8. You have flexible housekeeping standards.

—Do you accept the proposition that the space under a person's bed is as good a place as any for an old peanut butter and jelly sandwich?

### 9. Privacy is a minor concern in your life.

—Do you feel that three people are not too many for a bathtub as long as two of them are small?

### 10. You have a motherly perspective on current events.

—Do you believe that a sudden outbreak of diaper rash ranks right up there with all the other sudden outbreaks in the world?

### 11. You can disguise a threat as a rhetorical question.

Can you ask the following as though the kid had a choice?

—"Are you looking for a spanking?"

—"Do you want your face to stay like that?"

—"Are you trying to ruin your eyes?"

## Can You Talk Like a Mother?

As a mom, you have an image to uphold. You are expected to be the repository of cliches for all manner of uncomfortable and distressing occasions.

So, quick, what's the rest of this cliche guaranteed to induce guilt in a sassy kid? "You'll be sorry when I'm . . ." If you answered "six feet under," you're ready to move on to the challenges below. Match the columns to complete the appropriate cliche for each scenario described.

COLUMN 1

Your kid threatens to run away. You say, "Good, I'll . . ."

Your kid tells you he wants a motorized skateboard like his friend Richard's. You say, "If Richard . . . would you do the same thing?"

Your child starts sniffling when you insist he eat his beans. You bark, "If you don't stop crying, I'll . . ."

Your ten-year-old lets out a sarcastic "Hah" when you describe the dire consequences if he doesn't start his homework now. You say, "If you think I don't mean it, just . . ."

Your child becomes so bratty, you are driven to spanking, but you ease your guilt by saying, "This will . . ."

COLUMN 2

telling you

abide by my rules

going without you

come here where I can hear you

I'm talking to you

# ARE YOU MOTHER MATERIAL?

| COLUMN 1 | COLUMN 2 |
|---|---|
| After seven "Are we there yets?" during a five-minute ride, you explode, "I don't want to hear another . . ." | **if it weren't tied on** |
| At 3:30 P.M. on a snowy day, your child comes through the door wearing what you recognize as his teacher's size large Patagonia jacket. You know what's happened and say, "You'd lose your head if . . ." | **peep out of you** |
| It's 3 A.M., and you are delivering your standard, "Don't-you-know-how-I-worry-when-you-miss-curfew lecture as your son examines his tennis shoes. You shout, "Look at me when I'm . . ." | **try me** |
| You are matching socks in the laundry room when an adolescent voice in the distance calls out, "Have you seen my frmgrtuztu?" You yell back, "If you want to ask me something . . ." | **pack your lunch** |
| You're trying to drag your family out to a K-Mart sale when your four-year-old dawdles. You threaten, "If you're not ready by the time I count to ten, we're . . ." | **hurt me more than it will hurt you** |
| When your daughter calls you a fascist because you want her home before daybreak on junior | **jumped off the Empire State Building** |

21

COLUMN 1

COLUMN 2

prom night, you say, "As long as you live in this house, young lady, you'll . . ."

Every night it's the same scenario. Bedtime comes and your child stays glued to the tube. Three times you say please, then let him have it. "I'm not asking you. I'm . . ."

**give you something to cry about**

---

"Motherhood is the most emotional experience of one's life. One joins a kind of woman's mafia."

—Janet Suzman, *The Observer*, July 1981

*(Good idea. Maybe now we'll get some techniques for disciplining kids that work.)*

---

# The Mother's Index

Let's assume so far so good. You have what it takes to be a mother. The question remains: Are you sure you want to be? Before you gush out an answer, take the time for a look at some hard, cold statistics, some of them disconcerting enough to have given even Ethel Kennedy second thoughts. Then we'll talk further.

Average number of yawns stifled by moms during school productions of *Our Town* in which their children are appearing: **13**

Percentage of store-bought cakes purchased for the first birthday of the first child: **10**

Percentage of store-bought cakes purchased for the first birthday of the fourth child: **63**

Percentage of mothers who give up after seven attempts to open a child-proof aspirin bottle: **60**

Percentage of children who will keep playing with the child-proof aspirin bottle until they find the winning combination: **65**

Average number of hours moms spend tracking down this year's hot Christmas toy: **19**

Average number of minutes children of these moms spend playing with this year's hot Christmas toy: **19**

Number of Saturday afternoons in a typical year mom reserves for herself: **2**

Number of these afternoons the kids get sick and throw up on three sets of sheets: **2**

Percentage of children who threw away little boxes of raisins mothers put in their lunches before raisins began to dance on television: **60**

After raisins began to dance: **15**

Percentage of moms who have given in to their kids' hounding to get a pet: **73**

Percentage of these moms who could kick themselves two months later: **98**

Weight of the average six-year-old in pounds: **63**

Weight of the average six-year-old whom mom must carry into the house from the car at 1:30 A.M. after driving through three states: **157**

Number of times mom bundles up the average kid against the cold and snow in a typical winter: **92**

Number of times the kid has to go potty when she's finished: **65**

Number of times in a lifetime a mother of three says, "Get dressed. Eat your breakfast. Pick up your toys. Say thank you. Pay attention.": **4,000,050**

Number of times one of these mothers feels she'll go bonkers if she says any of these things one more time: **4,000,000**

Odds that a movie to which an eight-year-old drags his mom will not feature a car chase: **1 in 19**

Number of times in a typical school year a child will be assigned to take in three dozen homemade cookies for a celebration: **6**

Number of times a child will forget this assignment until the morning of the celebration: **5**

# 2

## Stages of Motherhood: A Mom-Spotter's Guide

It's corny, but it's also true. A secret bond exists between all the mothers of the world. One mother of a preschooler will be able to recognize another woman coming down the street as also belonging to the sisterhood of preschool moms, even though the kids are nowhere in sight.

The mother of a teenager will spot the mother of an elementary school kid because she once had a kid that age herself.

How do moms work this magic?

The technique is really as much a science as an art. The illustrations on the following pages will help you hone your own skills as a mom spotter.

# Baby's First Year

Eyes permanently at half-mast

Dark roots showing. She'll color it if she ever goes out again.

Perpetually soggy shoulders

Easy-open blouse for frequent feedings

Romance novel substitutes for sex life

Club Med tote bag now serves as diaper dispenser

Fifteen extra pounds here she dreamt of losing before she got pregnant

# The Terrible Twos

Short haircut less vulnerable to tangles from Goofy Glue

Sand in ears is from the playground, not Waikiki

Hasn't said no so often since her high school dating days

Vocal cords have begun to rival Pavarotti's

SHOW&TELL
A NEW AGE GUIDE TO TOILET TRAINING

Library book eight months overdue

Relaxation tapes undone by two-year-old curiosity

Nasty note from neighbors regarding that Play Doh in their petunias

# Nursery School Years

New hairdo is to impress those in her new social circle—teachers and car pool mothers

Worried about whether a kid who says "pasghetti" will make it in academia

Secret chocolate chip cookie recipe to remind kid there are some things he can't get OUT THERE

Clear eyes, thanks to the uninterrupted nap she's dreamed of for five years

Smudges from overseeing the first finger-painting project

Full skirt affords child a safe haven from the UNKNOWN

Wanted a BMW but settled for a ten-year-old station wagon to carpool eight kids and a dog

# Elementary School Years

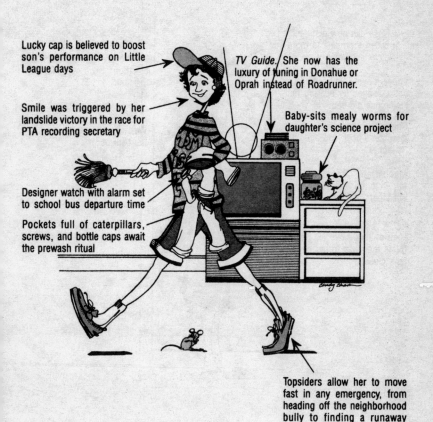

Lucky cap is believed to boost son's performance on Little League days

Smile was triggered by her landslide victory in the race for PTA recording secretary

Designer watch with alarm set to school bus departure time

Pockets full of caterpillars, screws, and bottle caps await the prewash ritual

*TV Guide.* She now has the luxury of tuning in Donahue or Oprah instead of Roadrunner.

Baby-sits mealy worms for daughter's science project

Topsiders allow her to move fast in any emergency, from heading off the neighborhood bully to finding a runaway pet rat

# High School Years

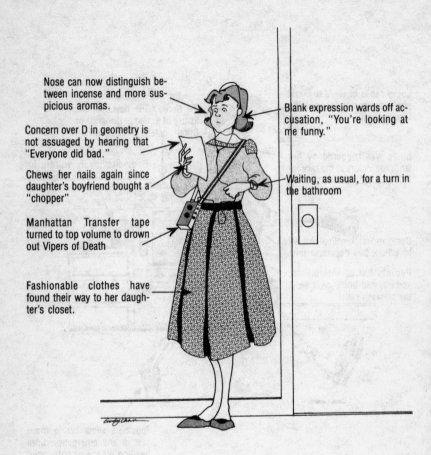

Nose can now distinguish between incense and more suspicious aromas.

Concern over D in geometry is not assuaged by hearing that "Everyone did bad."

Chews her nails again since daughter's boyfriend bought a "chopper"

Manhattan Transfer tape turned to top volume to drown out Vipers of Death

Fashionable clothes have found their way to her daughter's closet.

Blank expression wards off accusation, "You're looking at me funny."

Waiting, as usual, for a turn in the bathroom

# College Years

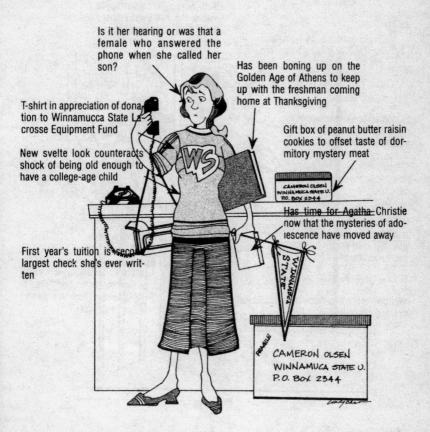

## Mother of the Bride

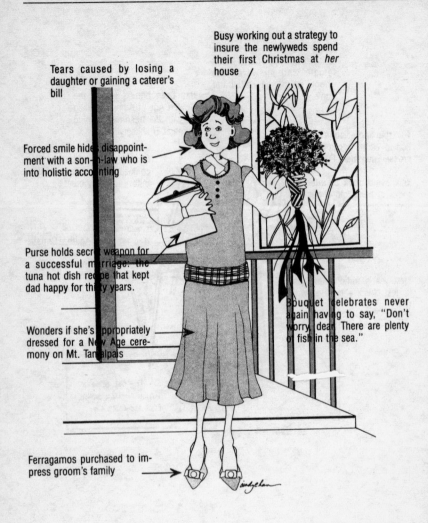

Busy working out a strategy to insure the newlyweds spend their first Christmas at *her* house

Tears caused by losing a daughter or gaining a caterer's bill

Forced smile hides disappointment with a son-in-law who is into holistic accounting

Purse holds secret weapon for a successful marriage: the tuna hot dish recipe that kept dad happy for thirty years.

Wonders if she's appropriately dressed for a New Age ceremony on Mt. Tamalpais

Bouquet celebrates never again having to say, "Don't worry, dear. There are plenty of fish in the sea."

Ferragamos purchased to impress groom's family

# Mother of Adult Children

Paints whenever she feels like it, since the chorus of voices yelling, "Hey, mom, what's for dinner" is now but a memory

Studies the social pages to keep track of who's married and who's still eligible in case her single daughter ever asks

Secret recipe for son's favorite lasagna that she conveniently forgets to give to daughter-in-law

Smiling because her daughter called to ask how to get wine stains out of a linen table-cloth—the first advice the girl has tolerated in fourteen years

Unlike most frequent fliers, she is motivated by love and distant children, not money and deal-making

Size 2 knitting needles—just the right size for knitting booties

# WHAT WE LEARN FROM THE KIDS #1

*Just because moms aren't as frantic to tell their personal stories as fading movie stars and political outcasts doesn't mean they don't have a lot to share.*

*Joking aside, there's plenty of motherly wisdom out there that, if properly packaged, just might give Dr. T. Berry Brazelton a run for his money.*

*But you be the judge. Here and elsewhere in the book are contenders in the Unofficial Mother's Handbook Essay Contest, writing on the topic, "What I Learned from My Kids."*

Patty was sixteen and rebelling against everything adult, including higher education. Still, during a vacation drive through New England, Jack and I decided to stop and walk around Harvard. We figured maybe the action on campus might impress her.

Wrong. She refused to get out of the car. "You guys go ahead," she insisted. "I'll just listen to music." And with that, she flicked on the radio to a station playing a song called "Sex, Drugs, and Rock and Roll."

That day I learned the value of choosing my battles.

I convinced Jack not to mention college to Patty again, and eventually she decided to enroll on her own (although not exactly at Harvard). More important, she was a more pleasant kid during the intervening years than I suspect she would have been if we'd stayed on her case.

The boys, who were younger, were the real beneficiaries of my new insight, however. I'd been having this running battle with them about taking care of their clothes. The deal had been that I'd wash, then it was their job to fold and put the stuff away—which, of course, they always conveniently forgot to do. Meanwhile, I was forever harping and sounding like a shrew.

One day I got sick of it. I went out and bought a huge wicker bin that I christened the Grope Basket. I told the boys I'd deposit their laundered clothes in it, then it was up to them. They could put the stuff away or leave it there and grope. I would nag no more.

Well, you can guess how often they put anything away. Right. Never. They groped for four and six years respectively until they, too, left the nest and then they found scrunched-up garments they'd forgotten they owned. Meanwhile, though, I had stopped being a knee-jerk nag, so when something really mattered to me—such as the time I told the oldest he could buy a moped only if he'd wear a helmet when he drove it—they knew I meant it, and they listened.

If I had it to do over again, I'd start choosing my battles a lot sooner. I'd tell myself: What does it matter if a five-year-old kid eats only burritos? I can always throw in a few vegetables and make it a balanced diet. My ten-year-old decides he wants to go without underwear? Fine. There'll be less laundry.

I'd save the hard-nosed "No way, Jose" stuff for precious few situations: things that might affect the kids' health or safety (or someone else's) or that would be cruel or a breach of manners.

I'd bite my tongue a lot. And who knows? Maybe some of the things I ranted about didn't matter in the long run. I noticed the craziest thing after the boys started dressing themselves from the Grope Basket. They'd be wearing things I knew had been wadded in that bin for weeks, yet they usually looked just fine. Of course, I would never go so far as to tell them that. I mean, there are limits, even to a mother's love.

"God could not be everywhere and therefore he made mothers."
—Jewish proverb

(Do you think he might be willing to trade places for a while? Mom could throw the thunderbolts, he could do the laundry.)

# 3

# *Mother Types: A Field Guide to the Species*

**M**ythology aside, the truth is that many moms have never said, "Do I look like your slave?" And a few have never even served a tuna casserole. Indeed, in that vast sisterhood of mothers, there is a lot more variety than you may think. The field guide to the species, which follows, catalogs some of this diversity.

## The WASP Mom

Order is important to the WASP mom. While she loves her little "Droopy Drawers" and "Prune Face"—nicknames of affection among the initiated—she also remembers fondly the porcelain-faced dolls she took care of when she was growing up—dolls that were quiet, stayed where they were put, and were not about to produce a massive bowel movement just minutes after the family had belted up for the weekend flight to Bar Harbor.

But the WASP mom has learned that real kids are full of little surprises like this, which is one reason why she has "a little help." And on nanny's day off, if things become too chaotic, mom has developed her own repertoire of tricks to entertain the kids and give her a few minutes to herself. In one game, for example, she throws Gummy Bears out into the garden and lets the children scramble for them. That little episode gives her a good fifteen minutes for aerobics or compiling a dinner party list.

The WASP mom's kids think she's great, though, not just because she hands out Gummy Bears so freely, but also because they understand her rules. There are no bloody battles in the WASP household over whether the kids will eat their liver. Mom gives a lot of room to children who follow a few basic guidelines. They are always, for example, to say "please" and "thank you" when begging between-meal-snacks from the cook. They must use the L. L. Bean catalog when making out birthday and Christmas lists. And so on.

WASP children who abide by these and a few other common sense principles of good manners learn that their mother won't hassle them much. That's because her instincts and tradition tell her that kids need a chance to "just horse around." Let those who need it sentence their ten-year-olds to SAT preparation classes. Her children already have the basics for getting ahead: a mother who attended Smith, a father who graduated from Yale, and a whole community of neighbors who know the difference between a flotilla and a regatta.

# The Jewish Mom

These days a mom does not actually have to be Jewish to be a Jewish mother. Any mom, for instance, who, through coaxing or intimidation, can nudge an eight-year-old into practicing the violin for an hour a day deserves at least a nomination. But, of course, the Jewish mom's talents are not easy to come by.

She understands, for example, that while a mother should never nag, she must frequently give direction. The Jewish mom would not expect her son to understand without a little help that, given two summer camps, both situated among whispering pines on the banks of clear mountain lakes, both with a full range of recreational activities, the one with five and a half hours a day of intensive computer programming training has to be the clear choice.

And what seventeen-year-old sees enough of the big picture to grasp that while "sexual dysfunction counselor" may seem like a fadishly glamorous career at the moment, the world will need good radiologists for a long time to come.

The Jewish mother also has a strong commitment to nutrition. Whether her children are trying out for the football team or the debate club, she knows they will be more likely to excel if beforehand they will just take the time to eat a little. And when scientists recently discovered that chicken soup really is good for colds, she said calmly, "Of course. One of these days, they'll understand it is better when you wash it down with a little bread."

The Jewish mother sees constructive criticism as a big part of her job. "Someday they'll thank me," she says. And she's usually right. One reason for their gratitude is that, regardless of what the Jewish mom has to say to her kids at home, she'll put on the best possible front outside the house. One morning she might be reminding her son, "Your cousin Milton didn't get into Harvard with A minuses." But later at Temple Social Hour with the other mothers, she'll say, "Ah, what a son. Just this morning, we were discussing his going to Harvard."

## The Catholic Mom

The Catholic mom has always thought that on one point the Church definitely has its priorities straight: All the kids learn to pray to a mother. Beyond that, it hasn't always been easy.

Her job, as she sees it, is to accentuate the negative, keeping her kids' mortal and venial sins to a minimum.

The basic stuff she can handle. She assumes, for instance, that her kids are not going to goof around in church. She knows that her laser-beam glare guarantees they will at least sit quietly counting bald heads and staring at other kids even while blocking out Father's message for moral uplift.

It's tough, however, steering her kids away from temptation in the age of Dr. Ruth. She tries to pass on the wisdom her mother passed on to her. Recently she gave her nine-year-old daughter her mother's advice that, no, the girl couldn't have a pair of patent leather Mary Janes for Easter—like the public school girls—as shiny shoes would be an invitation for boys to look up her dress in the reflection. The child didn't argue, of course, but looked at the Catholic mom as if the woman were a least bit deranged.

And when her eleven-year-old son wants to know what to do about "impure thoughts," the Catholic mom is not about to handle that one. She just ships the child off to Father Riley, who instructs him in how it is possible to obliterate licentious fantasies by substituting mental pictures of St. Sebastian being pierced with arrows and beaten to death and thrown into a sewer.

The Catholic mom has raised enough kids so that she knows what to expect. The preschoolers who take turns balancing on her knee and handing her the corn kernel markers for Friday night bingo cards will grow into adolescents who need some freedom. At which time, of course, they will be allowed to attend functions such as the postgame victory dance at Our Lady of Mount Carmel High. The Catholic mom expects that the imposing presence of Sister Mary Catherine as a chaperone on these occasions will be enough to remind the celebrants that their bodies are temples of the Holy Ghost.

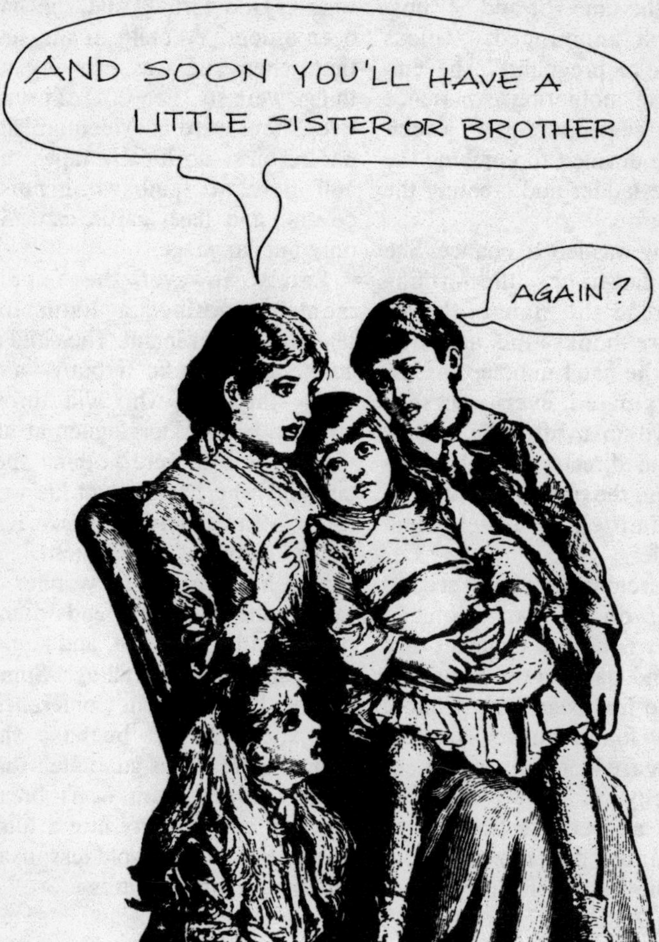
AND SOON YOU'LL HAVE A
LITTLE SISTER OR BROTHER
AGAIN?

# The Yuppie Mom

From the time she and her husband first announced, "Guess what. We're pregnant," she embraced the mothering experience with the same pursuit of excellence she devoted to climbing the corporate ladder and creating the perfect pesto.

Nothing was left to chance. She and the dad-to-be, "the birthing team," read the state-of-the-art child care books and attended state-of-the-art Lamaze classes. They evaluated every nursery school within a fifty-mile radius, asking the directors tough questions about the percentage of graduates admitted to Ivy League universities.

Each evening, from the second trimester on, Mozart replaced Huey Lewis on the compact disc player, and dad, whose idea of a good read had been early Elmore Leonard, found himself reciting Shakespeare sonnets to an enlarged belly.

It was all because the Yuppie mom wanted for her child all which she herself hadn't had. It wasn't, God forbid, that she had been a deprived child. It was just that when she was growing up things were so . . . well . . . primitive. There were no Valentino signature bibs, no lullaby tapes, no 100 percent lambswool potty covers, and flash cards came in only one language.

Lately, however, the Yuppie mom has noticed a disturbing tendency in her infant. The child is acting almost like a baby—any baby—the kind who will throw strained boeuf bourguignon at his mother as if it were nothing special and who has teethed his way through three sets of Super Kid Flash Cards (Infants Edition).

She has started to wonder if maybe she and her friends aren't pushing a bit too hard, and sometimes she thinks of calling a Super Parents Disarmament Conference. But she hesitates because she knows there is no guarantee that some nervous mom won't break the pact and secretly hire a tutor to give her four-year-old lessons in biophysics for beginners.

## The Sixties Mom

For her, the revolution is now a memory: the exhilaration of dancing under a light show at the Fillmore with little Jade strapped to her bosom; the steely glares of the playground mothers who seemed to find in the sight of her child's two-year-old sand-covered genitals a symbol for all that had turned decadent in the western world; the fights with the school principals and teachers about whether an absence to protest the illegitimate Vietnam War was "legitimate."

Actually, she didn't go into the revolution with a lot of theory. She simply decided she couldn't go wrong doing the opposite of everything her mother had done. Because her mother had taken her to see *Bambi,* she kept her kids away, concocting some now-forgotten rationale to explain why Walt Disney was not politically correct.

Her problems began when her kids became backsliders in the cultural revolution, a trend she became aware of when Jade asked her if she would mind, please, shaving the hair underneath her arms as it embarrassed the girl in front of her friends. After that, lots began to change, and the works of Carlos Castaneda were not much consolation when she had a teenage son out tooling around at 3:30 in the morning in someone's souped-up Chevy.

She has just returned from a trip to the mall with her daughter, who tried on seven hundred prom dresses before deciding on the first one, a ritual the sixties mom viewed with the fascination of a Margaret Mead watching Samoans come of age.

The sixties mom knows there will be no merry prankster bus for these kids, that her daughter will be going to the prom in a limousine of the sort that in less indulgent times was reserved for funerals and presidential inaugurations. But she also knows that she's shown them there's more to life than collecting Rolex watches and Mazda X cars. She is hoping that, in some part of them, Woodstock lives.

# The Working Mom

The calls usually come when the assistant to the vice-president for international development is sitting across the desk from her. But the working mom still listens calmly as her eight-year-old daughter asks if it's OK to put the hamster, who has fallen into the soup, in the oven to dry off.

Of course, the working mom doesn't allow her mothering to interfere with her job performance. But beyond that, she never hides the fact she's a mom. On the contrary, she wears the cereal stain on her skirt for what it is: a combat ribbon valiantly earned while caught in the crossfire breaking up a soggy Froot Loop war at breakfast.

She does not need to be a card-carrying member of the National Organization for Women to understand that life for the working mom is an ongoing battle. So when it comes to running her household, her style is less Molly Goldberg than it is Supply Officer for the 42nd Airborne. On Saturday, she makes and freezes enough cheese sandwiches to feed much of the population of Cameroon. On Sunday, she washes so many clothes that nobody can plan on a hot bath before next Tuesday.

The working mom may take an occasional chance on a lottery ticket, but she is not about to gamble on a no-show baby-sitter. Her Rolodex, a catalog of backup sitters for her backup sitters, lists so many fifteen-and-a-half-year-olds she could run a dating service at Soph Hop time.

Like just about everyone else who works, the working mom is doing it because she and her family need the money. She won't deny there are perks, however: It's nice to eat lunch with people who don't mash bananas into their nostrils. It's an upper to be with folks who can go for a whole day without whining, "We're bored."

Yes, a job can be seductive, but the working mom doesn't have trouble sorting out what's important. It's true her kids cannot provide her with a profit-sharing arrangement and a good dental plan. But Mother's Day will come and go and she will never receive from the company's director of human services a big hug and something cute made of popsicle sticks and painted macaroni.

# The Single Mom

You might have seen her at the county fair. Like any other fairly sane adult, she'll stagger from her four minutes in the clutches of the Whirligig Whiplash, wondering how she ever got snookered into this form of voluntary torture. Then comes the yank on the sleeve and the squeal, "Hey, mom, let's do it again," and she'll find herself weaving back toward the ticket booth propelled by the little voice that keeps saying: Single moms try harder.

Of course, it's true. Back in the days when there was a two-parent division of labor, she just drove the carpool to Little League games. Now she rotates the tires and packs the front wheel bearings on the car that gets the kids there and warms up the pitcher's curve ball once they arrive.

Not that she's bitter about the divorce, although it does bug her that there are all these sitcoms these days featuring dads raising kids in their spare time as though it were no more trouble than raising radishes. And another thing: Why is it that in this joint custody arrangement she's the one who coaxes the kids into eating their peas while their dad feeds them Doritos for breakfast?

But don't get the impression that she isn't still interested in men. On the contrary, she is always looking. It's just that she has a different checklist these days. It used to be: Does he have the business acumen of Donald Trump and the looks of Robert Redford? Now it's: Does he know the rules to Chutes and Ladders and the words to 'I'm a Little Teapot'?"

Any mating ritual that takes place these days is likely to be directed by committee. Primping for a date, she'll need to be prepared for some kibbitzing by a line-up of pint-sized fashion mavens who can't agree whether this time out she should look more like Cher or Bea Arthur.

An active social life, however, is seldom the single mom's top priority. These days when her fantasies are in high gear she is not thinking about a weekend on Antigua with Harrison Ford. She is thinking about coming home from work and hearing her kids say, "Mom, we can tell you're all tired tonight. We'll just go to bed early."

# 4

## Mothers Through the Years

*Continents shift and drift, nations rise and fall, but mothers keep on keeping on. Motherhood, most experts agree, is here to stay. Hence the inevitable questions: "Where have we been?" "Where are we going?" and other matters usually reserved for early-Sunday-morning talk shows.*

## Great Moments in Mothering

Of course, a great moment in mothering history is occurring right now as you read these words. At this very second, women all over the world are giving birth.

Since it is impossible to record all these major events in mothering history, this timeline is limited to spotlighting some moms who had good press agents and to documenting some breakthroughs (or breakdowns, depending on your point of view) along the way.

Mom of Abel and Cain mediates first bout of sibling rivalry.—**A very long time ago.**

Medea responds badly to first recorded case of colic.—**Not quite so long ago.**

Mother Goose discovers, to the delight of future moms everywhere, that little rhymes about muffets and tuffets will put kids to sleep.—**1719**

Queen Victoria conceives a child the Victorian way. Advises moms: Just close your eyes and think of England.—1840

In the interest of art, Mrs. Whistler sits still, letting lunch dishes pile up.—**1871**

Telephone invented. Sixteen-year-olds hail communications miracle; moms left speechless.—1876

Freud dreams up Oedipal theory, leaving mothers everywhere nervous about jumping out of the tub without a towel.—**1899**

First Mother's Day established—a day when kids cook breakfast while Hallmark and mom clean up.—1913

Ma Barker is first working mother to say, "I want it all now."—**1928**

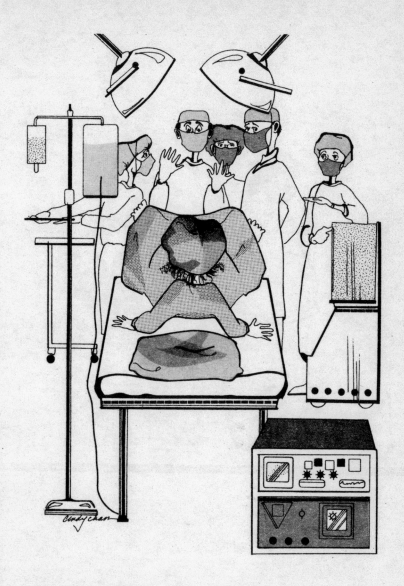

First hospital birth—Moms start paying big bucks to do what used to come naturally.—1930

Lamaze classes formed to teach moms more of what used to come naturally.—1950

Moms nominate first male for baby-sitter of the year—Captain Kangaroo.—1955

# Mothering: Then, Later, and Now

Mothering used to be simple and manageable. Then experts came along and things got complicated. Now mothering requires the logistical skill of a commanding officer at D-Day. Witness the evidence.

| What Mother Needed Then | What She Needed Later | What She Needs Now |
| --- | --- | --- |
| Grandma | Dr. Spock | A complete library of advice books with titles like *Bringing Up Diarrhea-Free Children in an Otherwise Messy World* |
| | A pediatrician who'd read Dr. Spock | A fancy neonatal growth and development specialist |
| | A kaffeeklatsch with other moms who'd read Dr. Spock | The phone number of a parental advice hotline |
| A blouse with buttons in the front | A starter supply of Gerber's Baby Gruel | A supply of fat-free, sugar-free, low-calorie, vitamin-fortified Cuisinart-produced Baby Gruel |
| The family rattle | A set of Lincoln Logs and a Parcheesi game | Designer flash cards |
| | | A Small Bytes Computer from F. A. O. Schwarz |
| "Heirloom" overalls | Off-the-rack overalls | Tailor-made overalls from Peek-a-Boutique |
| A shovel and pail | Three thousand Lego blocks | A creative play structure custom designed by Backyard Fantasies |

## Mothers in the Movies

Those mothers who want to cling to their Hallmark image of motherhood had better be selective about the movies they see. The stars may thank their moms on Academy Award night, but the moms they play on screen seldom spend their days baking cakes and pouring apple juice. Can you match these famous movie moms with their caricatures?

Rosalind Russell
as the mother in *Gypsy*
•
Shirley MacLaine
in *Terms of Endearment*
•
Faye Dunaway
in *Mommie Dearest*
•
Ellen Burstyn
in *The Exorcist*
•
Dumbo's mom
•
Mia Farrow
as Rosemary
in *Rosemary's Baby*
•
Teri Garr
in *Mr. Mom*
•
Anthony Perkins
in *Psycho*
•
Anne Bancroft
as Mrs. Robinson
in *The Graduate*
•
Katharine Hepburn
in *On Golden Pond*

This mother and her son were truly inseparable.

This mom must have had to look all over Manhattan for a baby cap with pointed ears.

This movie mom lost her hard-earned title to the Schooner Tuna Fish account.

This pushy mom took the clothes off her daughter's back.

This mom always enjoyed it when her daughter's friend slept over.

If it hadn't been for divine intercession, this mom could have spent a fortune on neck braces.

In this mom's hands, Dutch Cleanser became a near-lethal weapon.

This mom was the high-cheekboned half of the lovey-dovey old couple.

This perfect mom demonstrated that a mother's love is all some kids need to take off.

The actress who played this bitchy mom might offer some consolation to the character: Better luck next lifetime.

Cindy Chan

# Some Modern Moms Who Freaked Out

When Sam Levinson said, "Insanity is hereditary. You can get it from your children," he was supposed to be joking. But if he had been looking for evidence to support his claim, these narrative studies could help him make his case.

While most moms described here have not, unfortunately, effected complete recoveries, they have been recruited for useful community work as den mothers, carpool coordinators, PTA membership chairwomen, and other jobs anyone would have to be crazy to take on.

---

One day Patsy Blair stared at the little rivulets of strained carrots mixed with spittle meandering down her fourth child's chubby cheek and snapped.

She checked the balance in her emergency funds bank account, smiled, and dialed the number of the "Rent a Yenta: We'll Do Anything for You That's Legal" service.

"I want to be wheeled in a giant perambulator around the park," Patsy told the woman who answered. "I want to be dressed in a silk nightie and a little lace bonnet, and I want to be sucking on something nice and warm in a bottle. I want to be fitted with nice thick lace-edged diapers so I can pee whenever I feel like it."

There was a pause at the other end of the line. Then the woman said, "I understand. We can do that for you."

"Wait, that's not all," Patsy cried. "In the park, I want to be propped up in the carriage and entertained. I want people to stand around and make goofy faces and say silly things like 'Kitchy coo' and 'Is itty bitty baby nice and comfy?'"

Another pause, then, "We can do that, but it will cost for the extra people."

"Wait, wait, there's more," Patsy responded urgently. "I want someone to give me a little fuzzy bunny so I can throw it on the ground. Then I want the person to pick it up and give it back to me so I can shriek with delight and throw it down again. I want the person to repeat this degrading maneuver a couple of dozen times."

"I see," said the Yenta.

"And one more thing," Patsy added quickly. "I want someone to feed me out of a cute little dish decorated with pink and yellow pandas so I can pretend I'd rather starve than eat.

"I want her to try to get me to take a spoonful for mommy and daddy and all our relatives and my dolls and stuffed animals. Then after I get tired of that, I want her to pretend the spoonful of gruel is an airplane. I want her to raise the spoon into the air, twirl it around, then yell, 'Here comes the airplane. Open up the hangar.'"

"That's a tall order," said the Yenta, "but we'll find someone to do it. Someone," she sighed, "who's been a mother."

---

When, on the occasion of her thirty-eighth birthday, Hilda Slaag once again found a collection of dirty undergarments in the middle of the family room, she decided to unleash her ultimate weapon: public humiliation. Let's see, thought Hilda, how these kids, so accustomed to stonewalling her efforts at sweet reason, would stand up against a campaign of half-truths, innuendo, and outright lies.

Rushing to the phone the next time it rang, she let go her first barrage. "No, Jerome isn't home," she fibbed. "He insisted on going with his father to the Barry Manilow concert. But you shouldn't tell anyone."

Next day it was Kathy's turn as Hilda told her neighbor with kids that a distant cousin had finally agreed to come to town to take Kathy to the junior prom. "He isn't much for looks, but he's an excellent chess player," Hilda said.

The appetite for kinky rumors being what it is, Hilda understood perfectly well what the repercussions would be when she asked the supermarket clerk if the woman knew how to wean a teenage boy from sleeping with a teddy bear.

But perhaps the most devastating blow of all came the night Kathy actually did have a date. Hilda greeted the boy at the door with a cheery, "Kathy will be right down as soon as she finishes stuffing tissue in her bra."

The poor kids did not know what had hit them when Hilda found them at their very own table in the school cafeteria with enough space around them to suggest that her son and daughter had become the adolescent equivalent of a nuclear meltdown.

Sitting down and pulling a pair of dirty shorts from her purse, Hilda smiled sweetly and asked, "Now shall we talk?"

---

Jenny Kinney always treasured the few minutes she got to herself now and then in the only sanctuary her home afforded—the bathroom.

When her kids were young, Jenny tolerated the occasional "Whoops-sorry-mom-I-didn't-know-you-were-in-here" breeches of privacy. But when her children hit adolescence, things turned topsy-turvy.

Carl, a boy who had once viewed water strictly as a commodity for filling fake carnations that would squirt innocent bystanders, now took three showers a day.

Brigit, a girl who formerly had to be coaxed into combing her hair, now spent hours staring in the mirror as though her reflection might one day reveal that elusive adolescent identity.

Jenny became increasingly paranoid and agitated. Then one day when she was unable to get into the bathroom until 9:24 P.M., she snapped. The next morning, she got up at 4 A.M., took the portable TV and a selection of magazines, and locked herself in the bathroom.

No amount of pleading could coax Jenny out—not Brigit's lament that without the mousse she needed to scramble her hair, she couldn't be seen in public—not Carl's complaint that he had just spent sixty-five minutes jogging and smelled like a wet raccoon—not even her husband's plaintive plea, "Jenny, I'm meeting a client. I have to shave."

"I'll come out," Jenny announced, "when you agree to my new bathroom rule."

"What rule?" The question came as a chorus.

"In the future," Jenny spoke slowly, savoring her words, "each person gets a half-hour of bathroom time for each completed chore. Since I complete, on the average, 213 chores a day, that gives me an edge, but I'm confident that if you all work hard, you'll catch up."

Silence. Then, "That's fascist," mumbled Carl. "Mom, if we agree to this crazy system, you'll end up having the bathroom practically all to yourself," yelped Brigit.

Jenny settled back into the tub, flicked the TV dial to the *A.M. Show,* and opened a magazine to an article titled, "Moms—How to Gain a Little Clout Around the House."

"That," she purred, "is the idea."

---

When Miriam McEwen's kids got up that morning ready to launch their usual battles over who would get to choose the radio station, Miriam was not to be found in any of the usual places.

That is because Miriam was hidden away in the basement washroom scrawling out words inspired by a dream of the previous night. In this dream, parents all over her hometown of East Orange, New Jersey, were getting a second chance: The city council had passed a law allowing mothers to hire their children instead of having them arbitrarily assigned, as was presently the case.

It may have been a dream but it

was enough to get Miriam going. Now in the washroom, she was dashing off one classified ad after another soliciting new kids.

"Attention, experienced children. We have openings for a few qualified kids who do not try to sneak away before completing their piano practice.

"Good allowances and benefits for ambitious young people who can convince us they feel no compulsion to report in a loud voice on the skin problems of their older sisters or to con their little brothers with the old 'I'll give you five pennies if you'll give me a dime' scam.

"We will consider teams of youngsters who can agree among themselves when windows in the carpool station wagon should be up and when they should be down.

"An equal opportunity employer, we are interested in speaking with older children who can provide references confirming that they do not consider sex a subject too dirty to talk about with their parents and that, while off at college, they have never bounced a check in order to buy the entire fraternity pizza after a beer bust."

When Miriam finally dialed the paper to place the ads, she talked with a polite young woman who told Miriam the paper would position the ads where they would be likely to get the most attention: right after "Exotic Pets for Sale"

and before "Funky Collectibles Wanted."

———————————

When June Henney was awakened for the two hundred seventeenth consecutive day by the cacophonous twangs of The Rhythm Pigs, she counted to ten and resolved to nag no more.

Heading for the bathroom, she picked up her daughter Pamela's white makeup and black nail polish and emerged minutes later with a new look and the expression of one who has decided: If you can't beat 'em, join 'em. June dialed Domino's, ordered a pizza (extra pepperoni) for breakfast, then called her friends and invited them to come over and watch *Sid and Nancy* on the VCR. "Maybe," she suggested hopefully, "we can get wasted."

Unable to generate any enthusiasm, June spent the day thinking about herself, combing the closet for drop-dead clothes, and reading Zippy the Pinhead comics.

When her children arrived home from school at 3:30, they noticed, among other things, nacho dip on the hallway floor and the sweet smell of incense. Finding June sprawled out on the bed, staring at the ceiling, Pamela whined, "Mo-om. What's going on?" June, with a level look, answered Pamela quietly. "All the other mothers are doing it," she said.

———————————

**81**

# WHAT WE LEARN FROM THE KIDS #2

I read the other day that the cost of raising a basic no-frills child to age eighteen has climbed to $134,000—as much as it costs to buy a yacht.

Well, no one ever said that mothering was easy or cheap. But the way I figure it, once you start to analyze return on investment, kids win over yachts, hands down.

Sure, when they were little, my kids tried my patience and wore me out. One minute they'd be gluing bubble gum to the bucket seats, and the next thing I knew they'd be peeing on freshly folded laundry. Once at school they hooked Mikey's belt to the flagpole pully and hitched him up. I was fit to be tied.

On the other hand, nobody else in my life ever squealed with delight when I walked into a room, or asked grandma fifty-three times during one weekend when I went away, "When mama come? When mama come?"

And nobody else, on those days when I was feeling bitchy and put upon, climbed onto my lap, looked me in the eye and said, "Mommy, I love you."

In other words, nobody else ever so completely made me feel like the most important person in the world. That's worth a lot more to me than a yacht.

After they got to school, my kids became too independent and too sassy all too soon. I'll never forget how pained I felt the day I asked my nine-year-old a question in front of a group of his friends. "What's it to you?" he answered—softly but with real defiance. I knew my boy was announcing his "readiness for independence," as they say in the psychology books.

Yet this same boy once befriended a neighbor's shy child who was terrified of starting school and helped the youngster through several difficult weeks. And once my husband was laid off just before Christmas and we had to tell the children, "This year Santa Claus will come for you but not for mommy and daddy." On Christmas morning, we found two stockings tacked above the fireplace, one marked "Mom," the other "Dad," each filled with little puzzles and packages of M&Ms. I was so touched, I cried. No yacht could ever mean so much.

When the kids got to high school, I spent a lot of time waiting for the car to come home, the door to close, and the phone to ring. Then when they went off to college, I realized my days as full-time guidance counselor were over and I was serving instead as an occasional crisis center.

But then something wonderful happened. Some of the tension that had built up during the kids' teen years—tension I now suspect was necessary to help the children break away—disappeared. Today they seem to really enjoy coming home to visit and to appreciate what we do for them.

Another thing. We're finding we have a lot in common. We like the same movies, hiking trails, and mystery novels. And we talk about everything under the sun, from how much television kids should be allowed to watch to nuclear war. We're still family, but we've also become something more: friends. A better investment than a yacht? You know you don't even need to ask.

"What the mother sings to the cradle goes all the way down to the coffin."
—Henry Ward Beecher

*(But look for some updated lyrics at about age thirteen.)*

# 5

## The Many Faces of Mom

**H**ere's some small consolation for those mothering days on which you feel so seeped in juice and cookie service that you wonder if you can ever again function in the outside world. You learn a lot from mothering that can be useful to you later in polite society.

In how many other occupations, for example, would you have a chance to practice your skills as a plumber, drill sergeant, nurse, umpire, bank teller, and international diplomat—all before 9:30 Monday morning? For a look at some of your other motherly responsibilities, read on.

# The Disciplinarian

Much discipline is just spinning wheels. The same old wait-until-your-father-gets-home threats just don't work after awhile. Kids are continually coming up with creative ways of misbehaving. It's a mom's job to counter with equally innovative tactics for keeping the little monsters in line. Check the most imaginative response to each of the situations suggested below. As all of these are more creative than the usual bed-without-supper stuff, there are no wrong answers.

**1. Your child has decorated an entire wall of the family room with a Magic Marker dinosaur. You should:**
- (A) Make him write 100 times, "I will not draw any more tyrannosauruses in the family room" and triple-check for spelling.
- (b) Tell him grisly stories about Vincent Van Gogh and Toulouse-Lautrec.
- (C) Move.

**2. Your seven-year-old pilfers 35 cents from his sister's piggy bank. You should:**
- (A) Give him a choice: Pay back his sister 35 cents or give her 35 big kisses.
- (B) Donate his baseball card collection (in his sister's name) to the Cooperstown Museum.
- (C) Take front and side view photos of the kid and send them to the post office.

**3. Your thirteen-year-old daughter has lost four retainers in five weeks. You should:**
- (A) Give the kid a good scare; make an appointment with Steve Martin.
- (B) Tell her about the study that shows crooked teeth inhibit the sex drive in women
- (C) Insist she 'fess up to her character flaw at regular sessions of Orthodontic Equipment Losers Anonymous. "My name is Angela and I am a loser."

**4. You catch your kid red-handed watching *Bloopers, Screwups and Embarrassing Moments* the night before his geometry final. You should:**

(A) Hide the TV dial in the drawer of his study desk—someplace he'll never look.

(B) Restrict his TV viewing to *The Life Cycle of the Banana Slug, Trobriand Islanders' Linguistic Patterns,* and other public television staples.

(C) Blackmail him with a list, addressed to his girlfriend, of his own personal embarrassing moments, such as the time he wore a dress to go trick or treating and said, "Hey, mom, I kinda like this."

5. **Your kid's broken-record response to your every request that he share, wash up, and talk nice is "I don't hafta." You should:**

(A) Turn the Cuisinart to the chop, mince, or puree setting, fold your arms menacingly, and purr, "Come here, dear."

(B) Wait until the kid asks you to give him milk and cookies or read *Make Way for Ducklings,* and say "I don't hafta."

(C) Tell him a story about the kid who said, "I don't hafta" too many times and was turned by a mean fairy godmother into a toxic waste dump.

6. **You pay your daughter her weekly allowance for cleaning her room, but your on-site inspection reveals she has simply reshuffled the moldy Big Macs, dust bunnies, and smelly socks. You should:**

(A) Call an archeologist and report the possibility of artifacts dating back as far as 1977. Invite him in to do a dig.

(B) Dump in a truckload of dirt and see what sprouts.

(C) Rent it out as a location for a documentary on "The Seedy Underbelly of America's Middle Class."

7. **Your teenage son comes waltzing in at dawn, bleary-eyed, and tries to laugh off his misbehavior with a weak joke about how he still has four hours to go until his 11:30 curfew. You should:**

(A) Summon up the always effective threat: "Young man, just wait until your father gets up."

(B) Turn him away, saying, "Check-in time at this hotel is 7 A.M. Your room is taken."

(C) Tell him it's too bad he missed a phone call from some disk jockey. Some radio station. Something about a prize of a date with Molly Ringwald. Something about having to be home to win. You don't know what station.

## The Buddy

Almost every mom comes to realize that once kids hit eleven, they'll accompany her on a shopping trip only if they can trail an uncontaminated five paces behind. Teenagers just do not want to admit they are related to anyone over nineteen.

However, some moms overcome this inexorable natural law to become their teenagers' buddies. They say it's not that difficult a feat if you keep up with what's happening. You must know, for instance:

- That Melanie is going to break up with Josh because he was kissing Pam in back of the Beanery after third period.

- That Randy Blast is quitting as drummer of Profound Intrusion to join the Hare Krishnas. (That's the religion, not the group.)

- That the best seats for throwing rice during the *Rocky Horror Picture Show* are in the sixteenth row.

- That there are at least thirty-seven ways to hide a pimple.

- That getting one's ears pierced is a symbolic act that isn't just about the possibility of wearing earrings.

- That for thirteen-year-olds Barbie dolls are out but teddy bears are in.

- That geeks fall into two categories: the nice geeks who let you copy their homework and the nerdy geeks who don't.

- That a car without a tape deck is as depressing as a television without an MTV hookup.

- That a saleslady peeking into your dressing room to see how you're doing with your bra is gross, but the hunks who ogle your bikini at the beach are super icy.

- That the main purpose of friends is to get a network out there to report back which buff guys think you are a fox.

- That the discovery by two fifteen-year-olds of the opposite sex that they both like their cheeseburgers medium rare is very strong evidence that they were meant for each other.

## The Shrink

Conscientious mothers interested in promoting their offsprings' mental health—not to mention avoiding the cost of child psychiatrists—used to watch for aberrations like twitches and tics. No more. Now moms need to know about things like heredity-environment interaction, cognitive developmental theory, and bimodal perception. How would you fare in these situations?

| Focal Behavior | What It Could Mean | What Else It Could Mean |
|---|---|---|
| Kid can't talk | Generalized hostility syndrome | Kid is only two months old |
| Kid kicks the cat | Suppression/displaced anger mode or feline hostility syndrome | Kid is a brat |
| Kid smears food on wall | Anal retention disorder or mealtime hostility syndrome | Kid hates broccoli |
| Kid has temper tantrums at grandma's | Displaced hostility syndrome | Grandma needs bifocals, sticks kid with diaper pins |
| Kid hits brother | Dominance episode/acute sibling rivalry syndrome | Brother put slug in kid's pants |
| Kid hasn't gone out for two weeks | Incipient agoraphobia/anxiety syndrome | Kid has a zit that won't quit |
| Kid doesn't do homework | Faulty self-regulation/authority conflict | Kid can't understand quadratic equations |
| Kid insists on eating dinner in his room with the cat | Attention deficit/alienation syndrome | Cat doesn't ask, "How was school today, dear?" |
| Kid answers questions in monosyllables | Psychosocial inertia syndrome | Kid has watched too many Sylvester Stallone movies |
| Kid hides *Penthouse* magazines under bed | Gender obsession/maladaptive stimulus substitution | Kid likes the articles. Really. |

## The Advisor

One of a mother's responsibilities, of course, is to act as a moral guide and educator. In theory, this may sound like rewarding work, but the theory does not take into account that the advice and information a mom wants to give is ordinarily not the advice and information her child wants to hear (and vice versa).

So mom's job as advisor can get pretty sticky. That's why you'll need a strategy. Rather than just stumble through an answer next time your child asks loudly during a church service why dad doesn't wear tampons, plan your tactics in advance. Here are some models to choose from.

## The Evader

The evader acts on the principle that, faced with a curious child, a mom is always better off postponing until tomorrow advice she would have to choke and sputter her way through today. She is the maternal counterpart of the *Meet the Press* politician—the one whose idea of an answer is, "A more important question might be . . ."

Evasion, however, is not every mother's gift. The evasive mom needs to be a fast thinker. Suppose, for example, you are watching a Woody Allen movie on the VCR. Like any normal five-year-old, your child picks up just the word you wish he'd missed, and asks, "Mommy, what's an orgasm?"

If you are a successfully evasive mom, you'll sidestep the question, saying something like, "Well, Jason, an organism is . . ." It's that kind of on-your-feet mental dodging and weaving that makes a first-rate evader mom.

This is not to say that the evader can't plan in advance. Some moms find security in stockpiling a collection of diversions: "Just a moment, Jason. Right now I need to make an emergency call to my hairdresser." Or, "You'll have to wait, Jason. I have to go baste the roast."

The successfully evasive mom knows that a two-minute diversion is like a month to a kid—just enough time so she can be confident he'll forget what he asked.

## The Traditionalist

The traditional mom gives advice without the footnotes of experts. Her source is oral tradition, and she has a collection of old wives' tales and hoary cliches available for any emergency.

Whatever goes wrong, she relies on the same advice her mother once gave her.

When some demented kid decides he would rather go bowling than escort her daughter to the junior prom, the traditional mom gives just the advice you'd expect. "Don't worry. There are plenty of fish in the sea." Then, a few well-placed phone calls later—lo and behold—a friend of the family home from college just happens to call asking if he can do the honors. This occurs minutes before the tux rental shop closes, just like in the old Andy Hardy movies.

The best thing about a traditional mom from a kid's point of view is that she can always be pretty sure of what mom is going to say. So when she calls from any place in town offering any excuse about why she has to "sleep over," she knows it's not likely she'll face the third-degree tactics employed by more modern and suspicious moms. Instead, the traditional mom will always have the same sound advice. "Wash your underwear. If you're in an accident on the way home tomorrow, you wouldn't want to be taken to the hospital wearing dirty underwear."

This is not to say that the traditional mom is oblivious to the hazards of modern life. She simply doesn't see any reason to use scare tactics when old-fashioned common sense advice will do. Thus, when her daughter wants to go with a friend to a punk rock club in a seedy part of town, the traditional mom doesn't dredge up horror stories from *The Daily News*. Instead, she says, "Not tonight, dear. A growing girl needs her beauty sleep."

---

"An author who speaks about his own book is almost as bad as a mother who talks about her own children."

—Benjamin Disraeli

*(So lighten up, mom. Just lay back and wait for the reviews in* The New York Times.*)*

## The Pollyanna

The mom who gives Pollyanna advice suffers a bad reputation that is not always justified. Sure, sex may be more—and certainly less—than "a beautiful expression of love between a man and a woman." But such a sentiment seems an appropriate enough foil to the Public Health Department safe sex guidelines, complete with graphics, that her twelve-year-old is issued in P.E. class.

Optimism is in rare supply these days, and for that reason alone the endangered species of Pollyanna mom should be appreciated.

She is the one who believes it's never over 'til it's over. She is not going to throw lamps around because Malcolm brings home a mid-term D in chemistry. Instead she'll tell her son, "You can pull it up. It's the final grades that count."

Then when Malcolm brings home a final D in chemistry, she'll say, "Well, you know, in life, grades aren't the most important thing."

It's this ability to grasp the big picture, no matter how out of focus it is, that's the Pollyanna mom's chief asset. When her daughter has her lunch money stolen again, or her son fails to make the cut for the soccer team, the Pollyanna mom lets her children know that these adversities hold a silver lining. Little catastrophes build strong character.

Okay, it might sound simpleminded, but it's advice that has coaxed more than one kid out of a seven-day blue funk and back to the dinner table fighting for the last second helping, another activity that builds character.

## The Realist

Ever notice those newspaper lists of high-stress occupations like stuntman, commodities dealer, and urban bus driver? For some reason, you'll never see on these lists the most stressful occupation of all: mom.

Maybe it's just that the jour-

nalists see no reason to belabor the obvious. Everyone knows that the day-to-day hassles of raising kids is enough to drive any mother this side of Mother Theresa thoroughly bonkers.

But help is on the way. The child care experts have finally discovered what real moms have known all along: The way for a mother to stay out of the loony bin is to choose her battles, lower her standards, and in general GET REAL.

Take the quiz below to measure your R.Q.—Reality Quotient. Put a check next to each item you could care less about.

It doesn't bother me when:

- My child chews on a cigarette butt he found on the floor of the subway station as though it were a cherry-flavored Gummy Bear.

- At dinnertime, my kids try to outgross each other with attempts at bathroom humor—as long as they eat.

- My kids refuse to eat dinner—as long as they don't gross me out with attempts at bathroom humor.

- My three-year-old neglects his Junior Yamaha Keyboard to spend rainy afternoons banging together lids of pots and pans.

- My six-year-old insists that french fries count as a vegetable.

- One of my daughter's slumber party guests asks for a bottle of Windex to clean our bathroom mirror.

- My teenage daughter calls boring any event that does not revolve around her social life or involve the equivalent of a real life Invasion of the Body Snatchers.

- My daughter devours "young adult" pulp novels that make Nancy Drew mysteries look like candidates for the Nobel Prize.

- My son reports the C+ he has eked out in ceramics as if it were an acceptance letter from the Princeton Institute for Advanced Study.

---

"A rich child often sits in a poor mother's lap."

—Danish proverb

*(Especially right after Christmas)*

---

# 6

# *Mother's Rituals*

$T$*here is the story of the psychologist mom who proposed the following experiment. Round up all the seven-year-olds in the world and put them in a giant corral. Shuffle them up and redistribute them, one at a time, to moms of seven-year-olds. Make sure no mother gets back her own kid.*

*Now when bedtime comes, what are the chances that each mother will be left with a kid who whines, "Please, just five more minutes?" The smart money says 99 percent. That's because we are talking here about a universal bedtime ritual, one of those homespun ceremonies that takes on a life of its own that neither mother nor child can much control. Your life as a mom will be chock-full of such rituals, some more pleasant than others.*

# Mother's Day

Mother's Day celebrations come and go, but Mother's Day gifts last forever—or at least they pile up until the next garage sale. If kids knew what moms really wanted, they couldn't do much about it anyway. But why not dream?

| What Mom Wants | What Mom Gets |
| --- | --- |
| A week under a palm tree in Bermuda | A tree sculpted from the sports page |
| A nightcap on the Via Veneto | A shower cap from last summer's vacation at the Holiday Inn |
| A wardrobe custom-designed by Adolfo | A card custom-designed on the back of a spelling test |
| A pair of earrings that will knock people's eyes out | A pair of plastic face-shaped earrings with eyes that pop out and jiggle |
| An African safari, complete with wild elephants | *The Big Book of Elephant Jokes* |
| A front-row seat for the opening of the Metropolitan Opera | A front-row seat for a backyard rendition of "I Want a Girl Just Like the Girl Who Married Dear Old Dad" |
| A whole day to herself | A Day-Glo "World's Best Mom" decal |
| A season's lease of a forty-foot cabin cruiser | A one-bath loan of a battery-operated Bubble Tubble |

# The Family Dinner

You aren't going to get a lot of help from Amy Vanderbilt when it comes to teaching your kids to eat. The right fork for the quenelles de poisson is not an issue. Instead, each night at dinner you are going to be called on to make split-second combat-zone decisions about just how much you can tolerate before you either throw in the towel or throw up.

Here are some guidelines that can help you figure out how much grossness you can withstand during the mealtime ritual.

| Acceptable | Unacceptable |
|---|---|
| Flipping a meatball into the air and catching it in one's mouth like a seal | Flipping a meatball into the air and, unlike a seal, missing it |
| Stuffing a whole bowlful of bread pudding into one's mouth | Stuffing a whole bowlful of bread pudding into one's pocket |
| Grabbing the last piece of pizza from one's sister's plate | Grabbing the last piece of pizza from one's sister's mouth |
| Whining "Where's the catsup bottle?" just after mom sits down for the fourth time | Whining, "No, not that catsup bottle. The Miss Piggy catsup bottle," after mom sits down for the fifth time |
| Describing the disgusting details of today's biology class frog dissection experiments | Producing the disgusting remains of this experiment |
| Filing the usual obnoxious complaints about yucky green stuff | Inciting a yucky-green-stuff, cup-rattling, mess hall riot like the one in the James Cagney prison movie on TV last night |
| Sticking out a tongue full of half-chewed hot dog at one's sister | Sticking out a tongue full of half chewed hot dog at one's mother |
| Pushing food around into little piles instead of eating and then saying, "I'm full." | Pushing food around into little piles instead of eating and then saying, "What's for dessert?" |

# Vacationing with Kids

Some moms see motherhood as a state of enforced hibernation during which excursions into the outside world are limited to forays in search of Similac, strained carrots, and Pampers.

Other more spunky moms insist that motherhood can be more than a twenty-year ticket to a domestic gulag. You may be among the moms who want alternatives.

However, before you commit yourself to an extended trip out of the house, be aware of the problems you can expect. A little advance knowledge is the all-important first step toward coping.

---

"A boy's best friend is his mother."

—Title of a song by Henry Miller

*(At least until she pulls out the baby pictures to show to his girlfriend.)*

---

# What Will Happen When You Travel by Plane

First off, your child will be assigned to a specific seat—say, Row 20, Seat B. However, if your child is like most three-year-olds, he is not about to accept such an arbitrary designation. To him humans are creatures who must jump, squirm, and climb, and the fact that a child is now twenty thousand feet above the earth will do nothing to cool these natural urges. The entire nonsmoking section will soon become his territory.

But do not expect that the Yuppie businessman who has carefully arranged himself and his spread sheets four rows up will find your kid's wanderlust particularly cute. The guy may have heard about the friendly skies, but he is not about to be overly cordial when your child climbs on his lap to demand a reading of *Where The Wild Things Are*.

Even if you should manage to keep your child in the general vicinity of his assigned seat, he will quite likely make his presence known with a stream of nonstop babble that could set a Guinness record for the number of words spoken over a three-hour period by a toddler en route to visit his grandmother.

And, of course, your child will not understand that those smiling folk who move up and down the aisle passing out juice and honey nuts are there to look after his needs. As far as he is concerned, his personal flight attendant is the same person who attends him on the ground.

Soon it will become your job to dig into the overhead luggage rack looking for the *Masters of the Universe Coloring Book* that may keep the kid quiet for a few hundred more miles, to untangle his bib from his seat belt for the nineteenth time, and to retrieve the bottle that he's kicking down the aisle before it disappears forever among the first class seats.

Do not expect that thin air will do anything to retard your child's outpouring of questions: How do we stay up? Does God live up here? Why can't I open the window? Are we going to crash?

And, last, do not expect that others will greet these questions and this general racket with anything like understanding indulgence. You are going to get dirty looks that will make you feel like the Hester Prynne of Flight 602 out of Cleveland. Faced with this hostility, there will be only one thing to do: Pull out a copy of one of those in-flight magazines, bury yourself in an article about "Elegant Dining in Albuquerque," and wait for those magic words, "Thank you for flying United."

# What Will Happen When You Travel by Car

First of all, understand that the song of the open road will call out one set of connotations to you (adventure, romance, intrigue) and another to your kids (confinement, boring sights, and hours of being stuck with sibling geeks who poke, try to out-burp one another and otherwise act vomitrocious).

To help you through the car travel ordeal, an entire industry producing automobile-busy-work activities has developed. These car bingo games and connect-the-dots puzzles will provide healthy diversion until one of your brood destroys the mood by cheating, making a face, or getting carsick. Figure three minutes per activity, tops.

But let's back up. Naturally, as an experienced mom, you were not so foolish as to pile your brood into the car without first performing the Long Trip Ritual. The Long Trip Ritual has three parts: (1) Sequester each child individually in the bathroom. (2) Turn on the tap water. (3) Demand, "Go, even if you don't have to."

This tactic usually works for all but one holdout who insists he just can't go. And indeed he can't. Mere running water won't do it for him. What he needs is the sight of a sign that reads, "Next Rest Stop: 50 Miles." Then he is ready to spout like Old Faithful.

Of course, you'll tell the kid to never ever do this again, but that won't help right now. The youngster will simply look pained, clutch his crotch, and moan, "Hey, mom, you gotta stop. I'm gonna pee in my pants." At this point, the other children in the car will chorus, "Oh, yuck. Get him outa here. Let us outa here."

Should you manage to finesse your way around this mutiny, the interstate is still going to be one long bumpy road, particularly if you are holding on to the naive hope that your offspring may show some subtle sign that viewing the Grand Canyon at daybreak is somehow a qualitatively different experience than watching a Cap'n Crunch commercial.

The only mountains the kids are going to get excited about are located in theme parks and have rides through the middle. The only waterfalls they will pay any attention to are the ones that have been featured on *That's Incredible* with some guy walking a tightrope over them.

One way to avert full-scale civil war is to resort to the Count the Cow Game. You may have to accept the fact that the Carlsbad

Caverns, Painted Desert, and Giant Sequoias will be one Scenic Wonder blur to the kids. But at least they may arrive at their grandmother's house knowing the difference between a Guernsey and a Holstein.

Sometimes, if you just go with the flow, the hypnotizing purr of tires on asphalt will transport your kids to some weird psychic place where they'll begin to discuss questions such as "When a bear hibernates, how does it go to the bathroom?" Their arguments will stretch on longer and get more disgusting and create a noise level louder than you will think you can tolerate. Nonetheless, you'll let them go on since their talk provides a respite from their favorite question—the one with the most depressing answer. "Are we there yet?"

---

"The hand that rocks the cradle is the hand that rules the world."
—William Ross Wallace

*(Then how come the hand's owner can't make minimum wage?)*

---

# What Will Happen When You Go Camping

A family camping trip is, of course, always a trade-off. On the one hand, in the woods you've got a chance to commune with nature, teach the kids self-reliance, and cement family ties. On the other hand, back home you've got a self-cleaning oven.

No contest. But they will drag you along anyway, turning a deaf ear to your complaints that if God wanted woman to cook, wash dishes, and brush the kids' teeth in the same twelve-inch saucepan, he wouldn't have invented Chinese take-out franchises.

You have a pretty good idea of what to expect. Mother Nature may just be jealous because she does not have an all-electric kitchen, but, whatever her motivation, you can be sure she is going to keep reminding you that Seedy Park Pines is not a suite at the Plaza.

Like any proud mom, she will send out her offspring to impress you. But here we are not talking about a kid stumbling her way through a Chopin étude. We're talking about critters who creep, crawl, and sometimes even act ferocious. Nothing will stop their onslaught. The child you douse with mosquito repellent so pungent he smells like a tomcat in heat will nonetheless wake up the next day with fifty-eight mosquito bites, for which the camp manager and armchair physician will recommend hourly applications of boric acid and hot water.

The hot water may come either from the water you keep boiling and boiling and boiling or from the convenient hot water spigot in the restroom of the Seedy Pines Cafe, twenty-four miles of hairpin turns away.

Then, of course, the day you plan a getaway hike to Lackamucka Falls, you can be sure it will rain. You will be reduced to reading forest fire prevention booklets to children whose collective whining will attract enough curious furry friends to compete with the opening scene from *Bambi*.

Eventually, however, nature will show mercy, and the weather will clear just in time for you to whip up a supper of pork and beans, after which the kids will gleefully gross everyone out with tasteless jokes, complete with sound effects.

But that diversion, too, will pass. Soon the brood will start complaining, "This place is boring. I'd rather be at a motel watching *Star Trek*." You will agree.

---

"The father is always a Republican toward his son, and his mother is always a Democrat."

—Robert Frost

*(Which might work fine if the kid wasn't a damn independent.)*

# What Will Happen When You Go to the Beach

Take a beach vacation. Let Mother Nature do the baby-sitting. Who needs an au pair who might disappear for hours at a time with some lifeguard? All that sun, sky, sand, and water will humble your kids while you transform yourself into the model in the Bain du Soleil ads and fantasize about the bronzed body you will take back to the Washington Township Community Park Playground.

If you can find nothing wrong with this picture, you need to get your contacts checked. Take a closer look and you will observe the laws of kids and beaches operating as inexorably as the tides in which the children play. None of these laws bode well for mothers.

## The Law of Accumulation

No matter how equally you divvy up the pails, shovels, inner tubes, sieves, and water wheels, all these objects will gravitate to the hands of the biggest, strongest, and meanest. Inevitably, much of your afternoon will be spent refereeing tugs of war over objects mass-produced from brightly-colored plastic.

## The Principle of Survival of the Weakest

If the toddlers in your ménage are going to survive this back-to-nature experience and return to civilized afternoons of apple juice and Bert and Ernie, they will need a weapon with which to strike back at their older and more aggressive siblings. This weapon is tattling. Here are three of its classic day-at-the-beach forms.

- "Eric is going in too far." This cry will come from a dinky figure jumping about frantically at the water's edge about a quarter of a mile distant. The tyke's cry of emergency seems to signal that Eric will next surface somewhere around the Bay of Bengal, if at all, but more likely means that if Eric takes about ten more steps, he will get his bathing suit wet. You now have the choice of trekking the quarter mile over 104-degree sands to investigate or forgetting the whole thing and risking three to five years for child neglect.

- "Eric buried Melissa so she can't breathe." Well, sure, it's true that Melissa has been known to hold her breath during her no-more-brussels-sprouts tantrums, but who's to say that she'll have that spunk today? Robert Ludlum will have to wait. You don't want the headlines to read, "Beach Mom Buried in Spy Novel as Child is Buried Alive."

- "Eric put something down my bathing suit." You are paying $450 a week plus a nonrefundable cleaning deposit to provide your brood with sand and water thrills, and someone is always trying to impose one thrill too many. While all about are baking away, engrossed in what one Jackie Collins character is doing to another in the back of some Rolls-Royce, you will be collecting seaside depositions concerning who put a jellyfish into Kevin's trunks when he was taking a nap. Remember, bitterness will solve nothing.

**Rule of the Persistent Why**

Your kids may cheerfully leave behind their Sunday school clothes and dishwashing chores, but do not hold out hope that they will leave behind their "why" questions. You may lather on the cocoa butter and loosen your suit strap and dig your toes into the sand, but it will be business as usual for these little "why" machines, who will inquire in loud voices, "Why is that lady so fat?" "Why do I have to wait to eat?" "Why can't I pee in the water? Daddy does." You just want an even tan and these kids want you to perform like Sandra Day O'Connor.

Faced with these inexorable laws, some moms just give up on the glamour. They coat their noses with white stuff, don clip-on sunglasses and big floppy straw hats, and wear large comfortable flowered sunsuits. They sit and wait and think about the day the last of their brood will be out of the house, at which time they will run away to Tahiti, hang out with the great-grandchildren of Paul Gauguin, and get baked all over.

# What Will Happen When You Go to Europe

They say that when it comes to culture, you can never start too young. Of course, the they in question do not have children and probably work on commission for TWA World Travel.

You, not they, are going to have to find a way to appease the snooty waiter in the Paris bistro whose command of English is just good enough to understand your son complain, "This food looks like vomit." And you, not they, will have to figure out what to do with a kid who will eat only pommes frites three times a day for twenty-eight days, even though the tour contract demands full price for all the youngster's meals.

You will probably feel obliged to introduce your child to museum culture. If so, don't expect the other members of your sightseeing group to be charmed by the kid's snickers at the sight of the dinky private parts on Michelangelo's statue of David.

You might as well anticipate, too, that the child's fragile emotions, which could erupt into bouts of depression over barely visible zits back in Wichita Falls, will be exaggerated on foreign soil. Do not be surprised if, when in Venice, your preteen grabs one of those souvenir switchblade knives shaped like a gondola and cries out like a tenor in *La Traviata*, "Here take this and kill me. Kill me."

There will be unexpected reprieves. Your youngster will enjoy climbing the Spanish Steps as the trek will enable him to work off some of the energy that has been building up from staring at too many stained-glass windows.

There will also be unexpected embarrassments, however, such as when the child inquires of the handicapped groundskeeper at Notre Dame Cathedral, "Are you the hunchback?"

Eventually, out of desperation, you will throw away all attempts to enrich the child. You will find a McDonald's and scan the international papers for an American movie where you can take the brat to shut him up. Unfortunately, this maneuver, too, will backfire. As you sit back, ready to finally relax, and the opening credits of the latest Chuck Norris movie roll off the screen, your child will discover, to his horror, that the sound track has been dubbed in Italian.

# The Christmas Letter

The writing of the annual Christmas letter usually falls to you-know-who, as though she weren't busy enough during the holidays. But no matter. At least this chronicle of the year's highlights gives mom a chance to express herself, brag about the brood, and maybe even make some friends a little jealous. Here is an example of the genre to emulate or avoid.

Season's Greetings from the Mercks.

It's been a big year here in Willard Hollow. Frank was named sales manager at the Rug Doctor Chain which has brought us new fame and fortune. (Krystal Carrington, move over.) Of course, you know Frank. He is so conscientious he now works day and night. I'm always teasing, "Hey, let's cut a rug ourselves once in a while." (Frank adores my wit.)

I have extended the hours of my Hot Couture Boutique (get it?), which the sports and fashion writer at the *Daily Gazette* has called "the hautest fashion breakthrough since spandex pants suits." Isn't that a kick? Bloomingdale's, watch out.

Melanie is becoming quite the talented young flutist. She gave a razzle-dazzle recital in June, which everyone adored. We were really touched at how disappointed so many people were that they had to leave after the first intermission. It turned out the Dental Hygiene Week Display was being held at the school the same evening.

We're thinking of enrolling Josh in La Prestige Academy. The tuition is outrageous, but, as they say, if you've got it, why not use it? The academy people have assured Josh that his leadership of the Willard High Nautilus Team (does he take after his dad or what?) will offset those silly disagreements with his geometry teacher last year. You know how rigid the public schools can be for creative students.

The Rug Doctor firm wined and dined Frank and me on a luxurious Hawaiian cruise in August, and when I met their employees, I was sure glad I've kept my girlish figure (or so everyone tells me). It turns out most of those salesmen Frank has to go keep tabs on every week are sales-*women*.

But you know me. I thrive on competition, so I threw myself right into the swing of things. I entered the hula dancing contest for wives and won for my age group (although the judges were astounded to learn I was over thirty). You'd have been so proud of Frank. He declined being a judge so he wouldn't be accused of influencing the vote. Instead he was holed up doing some boring work with one of his new salespersons.

The crowd was wonderfully friendly. They even appointed me co-hostess of the going away luau, where I was in charge of giving out the leis. It was a lot of fun.

We hope you and yours had a wonderful year, too.

Tammy, Frank, and the kids

# WHAT WE LEARN FROM THE KIDS #3

I went into motherhood thinking I'd be a fountain of maternal wisdom. I pictured myself dispensing motherly advice to my kids at just the right moments to help them confront the challenges of growing up: sandbox bullies, advanced geometry, unrequited love.

Later, as I saw it, at least one of my children would tell Johnny Carson's audience, "I owe it all to my mom," and quote a few of my truisms.

Well, it didn't take me long to learn that real kids facing real catastrophes (or even imagined ones) want platitudes about as much as they want a comforting meal of brussels sprouts and liver.

When Stephanie was nearly three, she drove me crazy coming into my bedroom in the wee hours with trumped-up excuses like a fake tummy-ache to get attention. I told her she was a big girl now and big girls sleep through the night. I tried cheering her up, pointing out, "Look, you have a pretty room and nice pink Dr. Dentons and lots of cuddly stuffed animals. What could be wrong?"

Then my friend Sheila, a mother of five, said, "Stop spouting off. Just sit with the kid. That'll do more to assure her nothing horrible is going to happen before morning than tons of so-called motherly wisdom."

Sheila was right. After I spent a couple of nights just holding Stephanie, she began confiding her fears of monsters in the closet and noises on the roof. I didn't argue. I just nuzzled her matted hair and said "I understand" and soon she was sleeping peacefully through the night.

I remember another moment of truth. My ten-year-old son came home from school one day with a face as long as a dachshund's. "What's wrong?" I asked. "Nothing," he barked. I was wise enough not to press the issue and later he told me he had been the last one chosen at recess for basketball.

My instinct was to protest, "That's not fair. You're a terrific basketball player. Those boys are probably jealous."

But I didn't. Instead, I said, "Oh, that feels terrible, standing there and watching everyone else get picked." I told him I knew the pain because it had once happened to me.

Charlie was so surprised that a mother could have once been the last one picked that his mood shifted immediately. He talked for a good fifteen minutes about how disappointed he felt, then asked for a brownie and went out to ride his bike.

I wish I could tell you that these episodes transformed me from a know-it-all to a model of empathy, but that wouldn't be true. And, of course, there are times when kids do need motherly guidance.

But I can tell you I keep trying to improve, and that every time I say, "Oh, that must feel awful" instead of "Well, you know, there's a lesson to be learned here," I know my kids grow as human beings. So do I.

# 7

# Mom's Photo Album

Look through mom's photo album. Toward the front you'll find a couple of pictures of her as a kid back in the olden days when people still dressed funny and had weird hairdos. Then there will be maybe one or two photos of mom as a cheerleader or with a prom date.

Chances are, though, that the bulk of the photo album will record mom's life with her kids, from the cutting of the first umbilical cord to the snipping of the last apron string.

During these years, mom's social life and her children are inseparable. Look.

Me and the lamaze girls do our chorus line kicks.

Julia and I share a power lunch and learn the true meaning of the word "sandwich."

My Bluebird troop prepares for
the Great Butterfly Chase.

Ready for a relaxing day at the beach.

My honorable mention at the PTA Bake-Off.

Madge and Betty help out at Jason's "Big Six."

Graduation Day at the K.O. School of Martial Arts.

The preschool board of directors discusses water play rules.

Moms turn groupies for first performance of "Drones In Heat".

The family has a hot time on a cold day.

# THE BABY SITTER: CRITICAL ADJUNCT TO MOM'S SOCIAL LIFE

Let us not give the impression that moms need to be strapped to their kids like mother kangaroos. With months of careful planning, it is possible to occasionally sneak out for a candle lit tête-à-tête with your husband at Lucky Pierre's. First, however, you will need to master the note to the baby-sitter. It should go something like this.

---

Hi, Heather. Here are some pointers for the evening. Jody won't eat if the foods on his plate touch, so be sure to leave at least an inch between everything. The baby needs her medicine at 9:24. She won't want to take it but you can try mixing it with apple sauce. Sometimes that works, sometimes it doesn't. Her father says if all else fails, mix it with some Old Crow. (Just kidding.) Don't be alarmed if Darwin acts like you're not here; we figure it's just a stage he's going through. Tell Melanie she can watch the Michael Fox special if she stops trying to feed the goldfish Chewy Jells. If Jennifer and Jody start fighting about who gets to use the real marker for Candyland (the others are lost; we use buttons), tell them to flip a coin. But don't let Alex get his hands on any coins. He tries to stick them up his nose.

Bedtime is 8:30 sharp. Jody sometimes gets up later to say he's hungry. Just ignore it. Jennifer will want you to read her favorite book, *The Monster and the Princess,* but skip the parts about the monster. Otherwise, she'll call you in every fifteen minutes to see if he's under the bed.

Feel free to relax, watch television, and eat anything in the refrigerator except the stuff that looks like bread pudding. It's a secret concoction Melanie whipped up for a science project.

---

"We never make sport of religion, politics, race, or mothers. A movie mother never gets hit in the face with a custard pie."

—Mack Sennett

*(And in real life only occasionally with a game marker, a plastic doohickey, or a fistful of strained turkey.)*

# 8

## *Jokes for Moms Who Need Them*

A grandmother is impressed that her married daughter is able to keep the grocery bill so low. "How do you do it?" she asks.

"It's easy," explains the daughter. "I just put Gilbert in the shopping cart and before I get to the checkout stand, he throws half the stuff out."

---

A four-year-old boy looks longingly at his friend's dog. "My mother won't let me have a dog for Christmas," he says.

"Maybe you're asking the wrong way," says the friend.

"What do you mean?" asks the boy.

"Don't ask for a dog," says the friend. "Ask for a baby. Then you get a dog."

---

*Mom:* When your little sister comes, we'll have to move to a bigger house.

*Kid:* That wouldn't work. She'd follow us.

---

This little girl comes home from school eating a lollipop. The mother says, "Where did you get the lollipop?" The little girl says, "Billy gave it to me." The mother says, "Well, why did Billy give it to you?" The girl says, "He said if I stand on my head, he would give me a lollipop. So I stood on my head and he gave me the lollipop." Then the mother says, "Well, he only does it because he wants to see your underpants."

The next day the girl comes home from school with a lollipop.

Her mother says, "Where'd you get that lollipop?" The girl says, "Billy gave it to me. He told me if I'd stand on my head, he'd give me a lollipop, so I stood on my head and he gave me a lollipop." Her mother says, "I thought I said you shouldn't do that because he just wants to see your underpants." The little girl says, "Okay, okay."

The third day, the little girl comes home from school with a lollipop. Her mom says, "Where'd you get the lollipop?" "Well," says the girl, "Billy asked me to stand on my head and he'd give me a lollipop." Her mother says, "I thought I told you not to do that because he just wants to see your underpants."

"But, mommy, I fooled him," the little girl says. "I wasn't wearing any underpants."

---

Angela is very excited because her paternal grandmother has just finished the seventh day of her visit.

"Great," says Angela. "Now mom can do her trick."

"What trick is that?" asks the grandmother.

"Well," says Angela, "mom said if you stayed a whole week, she'd climb the walls, and I've never seen anyone do that before."

---

Mom to Dad: Can you take the kids to the zoo today?

Dad: I should say not. If the zoo wants them, let them come and get them.

---

Census taker to mom on the firing line. "No, no. I need the exact number of dependents, lady, not how many will still be alive after their father gets home."

---

Three proud mothers were discussing their eight-year-old sons.

"I just know my little Johnnie is going to be an engineer," says the first. "Whenever I buy him a toy, he tears it apart to see what makes it work."

The second mom says, "I'm so proud of Freddie, I just know he's going to be a great attorney. He argues with the other kids all the time."

"No question about it," says the third mother, "little Harold is destined to be a doctor. Why, he never comes when I call him."

---

A mother has guests and is eager to show off her son, David. She summons the boy.

"Tell us who was the first President of the United States."

"George Washington, mama," the boy answers smartly.

"And, David," his mama says,

"tell us, how do you spell *hippopotamus?*"

"H-i-p-p-o-p-o-t-a-m-u-s, mama." All the ladies sigh with admiration at the precocious child.

"But," the proud mama raises both hands, "you haven't heard anything yet. David," she whispers, leaning close to her son's ear, "Davy, say something to us in algebra."

---

*Mother:* When that naughty boy threw stones at you, why didn't you call me instead of throwing stones back at him?

*Practical-minded kid:* What good would that do? You couldn't hit the side of a barn.

---

The son, who is ranting about the importance of ecology, yells, "I can't stand all the dirt, pollution, and trash."

Mom says, "Okay, so let's get out of your room and talk someplace else."

---

*Mom:* Melissa, there are two words I don't want to hear from you ever again. One is "gross" and the other is "awesome."

*Melissa:* For sure, mom. What are they?

---

*Teenager #1:* I'm really worried. My mom works every day so I'll never want for anything and so I can go to college. Then when she gets home, she washes, irons, and cleans up after me, and she takes care of me when I'm sick."

*Teenager #2:* So what are you worried about?

*Teenager #1:* I'm afraid she might try to escape.

---

A woman went into the doctor's office and asked for a prescription for birth control pills. The doctor was a bit surprised because she was about sixty years old, and asked her why. She said they made her feel better and helped her go to sleep. The doctor asked how they did that. The woman answered, "Well, I crush them up and put them in a glass of orange juice and then put it in the refrigerator. Then I go to bed, but I toss and turn until my daughter comes home, opens the refrigerator, and drinks the orange juice. Then I feel better and go to sleep."

---

*Daughter* (home from college): I'm thinking of taking laundry service next semester if that's okay with you.

*Mother:* Honey, if you can get credit for it, and if you think you can pass it, take it.

---

A California woman calls her mother in New York and says, "Guess what, mom. I'm going cross-country skiing."

"Great," replies the mother. "When you get to New York, call, and we'll have dinner."

---

There was this young Jewish guy from New York and he went to California to practice law. It took a couple of years before he made it back to Brooklyn. One day he knocked at the door to his house and his mother hardly recognized him, all decked out in Gucci and Pierre Cardin.

"Well," she said, "I hope you still celebrate the Sabbath."

"Well," said the son, "actually, in California, most people go to the beach on the Sabbath."

"Oy, and the food, I hope you're eating kosher."

"Gee, mom, it's too much trouble to be kosher in California," said the son.

By this time the mother was ready to faint. She looked at him intently and said, "Tell me, son, tell your old mother, are you still circumcised?"

---

Three mothers are boasting about their son's affection for them.

The first says, "Have I got a son. The minute snow falls, he flies me off for two weeks in Palm Springs. He puts me up in the best hotel and pays the bill."

The second mother says, "Pardon me for saying it, but my son is even more considerate. The minute snow falls, he flies me off to Miami and gets me a private house on the beach."

The third mother, not to be outdone, says, "No question. You have two lovely boys. But my son. Well, what my son does is this. Every week he goes to a man and pays eighty dollars. For what? Just so he can lay down on a couch and talk. And what is my son talking about at such fancy prices? Me."

---

"In the last resort, men fight to impress their mothers."
—Gabriel Fielding

*(You mean it has nothing to do with wanting some other kid's Tonka tractor?)*

## WHAT WE LEARN FROM THE KIDS #4

You hear a lot about the importance of spending quality time with kids, but if you ask me, I'd say we need more idiot time with our children. I'll admit I'm not exactly sure what quality time is, but somehow the formal sound of it turns me off. I picture somber-faced moms reading *Blueberries for Sal* to a group of fidgety kids who would rather be out making mud pies.

Somehow the social scientists are making mothering about as much fun as going to the dentist.

I say we should listen less to the experts and more to our kids, and we'll all have a lot more fun.

Last week at the park my two-year-old saw his first worm. He jumped up and down and pointed as the tiny creature slithered through the dirt, and I realized how much kids help grown-ups take a fresh look at life.

When you stop to think of it, what's more invigorating than sharing with a child the excitement of discovery: the astonishment of first seeing fireflies or a giraffe or the pride of nursing a tadpole until it grows into a baby frog.

There's also the fun of sharing a child's simple achievements. I remember the day my oldest son, using a grown-up voice, told the dog to sit, and the animal actually sat. My son and I wore ear-to-ear smiles for the rest of the afternoon. I remember the evenings I giggled to myself listening to my daughter hunkered down under the covers learning to snap her fingers.

Of course, kids' silliness can get out of hand. I could manage a grin at the sight of three children sporting straws in their noses at the dinner table. But then when they egged the youngest one into putting apple sauce in his ears, that was too much.

But, on balance, I have learned that when life gets dark and scary and I find myself evaluating things, I never think, "I wish I'd fed my children more peas." Instead, I think about the picnics and the joy of watching them open just-what-they-wanted presents, and the thrill of receiving a Mother's Day gift of Mickey Mouse ears so I could play along with them in their backyard "Disneyland."

These are reason enough, I figure, to give family idiot time due respect.

# PLUME TICKLES YOUR FUNNYBONE

**MAXINE!** by Marian Henley. The first cartoon novel featuring the fabulous feminist and flirt, Maxine. Through her disasterous affair with the debonair T.S. Maverick and her tortured and hilarious recovery, Maxine always follows one rule—never, under any circumstances, remove your sunglasses! "Chonicles the inner flights of fancy and frenzy taken by one thoroughly modern woman." —*Utne Reader* (259991—$6.95)

**THE WIT AND WISDOM OF MARK TWAIN** edited by Alex Ayres. An A to Z compendium of quotes from the greatest American humorist-philosopher. This delightful new anthology has collected the best of Twain, his most trenchant—or most outrageous—quips, sayings, one-liners, and humor—not only from his beloved novels, but from his speeches, letters, and conversations. Arranged alphabetically by topic, from ADAM to YOUTH, here you will delight in sayings as fresh as when Twain first coined them. A wonderul book for browsing . . . or for reading and laughing out loud! (009820—$7.95)

**HOLLENHEAD** by Sabin C. Streeter. From the happily dog-eared pages of the *Yale Daily News* comes this hilarious send-up of the college scene. "In the world of art, precocious talent is a rare commodity. Among the chosen few is Yale's Sabin Streeter, a comic strip creator extraordinaire." —*Interview* (259541—$5.95)

**THE OFFICIAL M.D. HANDBOOK** by Anne Eva Ricks, M.D. Are you M.D. material? Find out with this hilarious handbook of tricks and secrets of the medical trade. Dr. Ricks offers an irreverent and humorous look at the life of a doctor, from med school to malpractice insurance. (254388—$4.95)

**THE UNOFFICIAL NURSE'S HANDBOOK** by Nina Schroeder, R.N., with Richard Mintzer. Find out what makes a nurse tick! Nina Schroeder will have you in stitches as she introduces you to the best and worse moments in a nursing career. From favorite nurse entertainment to famous phrases they teach in nursing school, the contents of this book are guaranteed to split your sides. (258995—$6.95)

---

**Buy them at your local**

**bookstore or use coupon**

**on next page for ordering.**